INTERIORS FOR COLLECTORS

John Phifer Marrs

INTERIORS FOR COLLECTORS

GIBBS SMITH
TO ENRICH AND INSPIRE HUMANKIND

First Edition

25 24 23 22 21   5 4 3 2 1

Text © 2021 John Phifer Marrs
Photographic credits on page 240

Published by
Gibbs Smith
P.O. Box 667
Layton, Utah 84041
1.800.835.4993 orders
www.gibbs-smith.com

Designed by Jeff Wincapaw/Tintype Studio
Printed and bound in China

Gibbs Smith books are printed on either recycled, 100% post-consumer waste, FSC-certified papers or on paper produced from sustainable PEFC-certified forest/controlled wood source. Learn more at www.pefc.org.

Library of Congress Control Number: 2021930716
ISBN: 978-1-4236-5686-9

Contents

Introduction   8

A Passion for Collecting   12

Collecting on a Higher Level
A Lake House Full of Collections and Family Keepsakes

Unique Collections   36

Victorian Silver
Art Glass
Silhouettes
Orange Fitzhugh
Antique Paintings
Parian Ware
Churchill Memorabilia
Imari Porcelains
Photography and Handbags
Chinese Mudmen

Building a New Home for a Collection   94

Inherited Furniture and Collectibles
Minerals and Geodes
French Antiques and Porcelains

Major Home Additions Just for Collections 146

A Family Wing in the Georgian Style
A Private Library and Art Gallery
A Southern Colonial for Art Collectors
A Residence for Entertaining with a Collections Wing

The Art and How-To of Displaying a Collection 206

Displaying a Collection
Installing the Collection
Arranging by Shape and Size
Background Colors, Fabrics, and Textures
Acquired Furniture Pieces or Cabinets for Collections
Custom Lighting for the Collection

Epilogue   238

Acknowledgments   239

Project Credits   240

Introduction

A book about collecting—how did that come about? Well, like many other designers who have been doing what they do for a really long time, I had friends who said, "You really need to write a book!" I would always pause and reply, "I think the last thing the world needs is another coffee table book on decorating!"

I didn't worry about it too much, but one day, as I was looking through photos of homes I had worked on, I became aware of all the wonderful collections that my clients had and how often I had organized, arranged, and displayed all those various collections. It was a part of the interior design that I loved and something that I felt I was good at doing. Some clients already had collections, but really didn't know it—so I would gather up the various collectibles from around the house and put them all together in a bookcase or organize them in a lovely piece of furniture or cabinet. Other clients collected passionately and I always had to find a spot for a new acquisition. Either way, I really enjoyed dealing with all these different collections and loved making them enjoyable for the client and attractive in their home. I didn't care so much what it was that they collected, or if I personally liked it; it didn't matter to me. My goal was to display the collection in the most attractive way in the context of a residence or home. I was amazed at how many collections I had worked my decorating magic on over the years. From small cabinets filled with porcelains to a private library displaying thousands of historical documents and artifacts, job after job showcased collections of wonderful things clients loved and enjoyed collecting. I was lucky enough to help them to arrange their collections to be lovely as well as loved in their homes. Hence, the idea for the book—*Interiors for Collectors*.

A Short History of Collecting

Why do people collect? That behavior has always fascinated me. I really don't know why people collect or what possesses them to collect, or if they even give collecting any conscious thought. Sometimes, it's just because they can and other times it's because they are so drawn to things—the shape, the color, the history, the rarity— that they cannot help but acquire more than just one. Sometimes collecting is kind of forced on them. Maybe they inherited a collection and felt the desire to add to it or maybe someone gave them something collectible and it got them started collecting a particular thing. One lady I knew had a collection of turtles. They were made of marble, glass, semiprecious stones, and even resin. I asked her how it started and she replied that someone gave her a turtle because she lived on Turtle Creek. Another friend of hers heard that she collected turtles and gave her several more and soon she had quite the collection. Later she told me, in confidence, that she really didn't care for turtles, but it was too late to confess. This is the perfect example of the forced collector.

I'm sure people have been collecting for as long as there was something to collect, or they finally had a break from looking for food and shelter. I imagine, long ago, a caveman found an unusual rock or piece of wood that looked interesting to him and he brought it into his cave and set it on the ground. Later, he stumbled upon a similar one and brought it home and soon he had a collection. He might even have carved a small base for the new treasures or organized them all on a shelf in the cave. I would not be a bit surprised! (Everything looks better on a custom base.) I'm sure the neighboring cave dwellers admired the collection, or perhaps envied it. That's okay too. A great collection does make one feel quite proud, if not slightly superior—even if we are just protecting and preserving the rare or unusual for the next generation of cave people. So, I suppose the world went along its merry way and people continued to collect whatever there was that was collectible—if they didn't need to eat it to survive. But enough of that.

Let's jump to around the seventeenth century where we find a Danish fellow— actually a physician and natural historian, by the name of Ole Worm (you really can't make this stuff up), who assembled a great collection of curiosities including preserved animals, horns, tusks, skeletons, minerals, interesting man-made objects, old sculptures, and even clockwork automata. These collectibles were all arranged in a room, or cabinet—as a room of collections was called in those days. These cabinets of the rare and unusual caught on but were limited to those who could afford to create and maintain them. People would travel great distances to visit these special cabinets. After all, seeing was believing—and since there were no museums, one had to know somebody who knew somebody who had one. Although there were numerous incredible items in these collections, many collectors couldn't resist outdoing their competitors in the rare and unusual department—sometimes claiming to have mythical creatures, or at least a part of a creature, such as the horn from a unicorn.

Gradually, the room of curiosities developed into just a single, but often fabulous piece of furniture, or cabinet, as we know it. These were often created from all sorts of exotic and expensive materials and designed to display a magnificent collection of the unique or possibly even monstrous. Someone finally came up with a rather brilliant name for these furniture pieces—cabinets of curiosities—the elegant great-great-great-grandfather, or -grandmother, of our common curio cabinet. So, don't look down on Aunt Gertrude's collectibles in her store-bought curio cabinet; it has quite the noble pedigree.

Most of these cabinets of curiosities were owned by kings and emperors, who loved to keep treasures locked up for their own viewing pleasure. They really saw no need to open their palace doors to share their treasures with anyone except, perhaps, other visiting royalty or worthy ambassadors, or presumed equals. This worked for a nice long time until the eighteenth century and the Age of Enlightenment arrived when nonroyals, or the commoners, wised up and got a little tired of doing all the work and not getting a piece of the pie—or at least getting a look at the pie! It was beginning to smell a bit like revolution—not pie. But hold on—nothing happened quickly back then.

Collecting in the eighteenth century was just as much in vogue, if not more so, than it ever was. What you wore, what you said, to whom you said it, and how you said it became as important as what you collected and where you displayed your collections—hopefully, in a grand home or even better, a palace. Everything was very serious and hidden behind a veil of manners where strict rules of etiquette and decorum ran the households of the rich and famous. Ideas about collecting and displaying a collection were advancing more than ever before. It was believed that a collection could be enhanced by being displayed, or viewed, in a beautiful setting—not just a single cabinet—but an entire room that held a collection of furniture, artwork, and accessories in perfect harmony. Secretive storage cabinets were out, and romantic, lovely rooms became the backdrops for magnificent collections. Beautifully planned and detailed rooms, where the furniture and decorative objects melded perfectly with the architecture, came to fruition in exquisite houses that held and displayed collections that had formerly been held in a single cabinet.

Many of these homes or chateaux or castles became our very first museums, after the royals went a little too far and lost not only their heads but their collections. After various revolutions, many private collections, and the buildings they were housed in, reverted to government ownership and were eventually opened to the public as museums. The people in charge of these institutions, or museums, learned to display, label, and classify the collections, as well as protect the collectibles from theft, loss, and decay. Museums curators also began assigning themselves the role of being arbiters of taste, as well as educating the public.

The nineteenth century brought in a world of rich robber barons and no income tax. Great fortunes in America were made by industrious individuals by the names of Frick, Hearst, and Morgan, to name a few, who could afford to collect whatever they wanted and build enormous residences in which to house their various accumulated collections, often ravaged from the dusty old grand houses and palaces of Europe and the former owners, who probably needed the money. Today, these are some of our most important museums and monuments and sources of pleasure, beauty, and knowledge for the collectors.

In the twentieth century, collecting became a hobby of not only the very wealthy but also the middle class. Vast numbers of everyday people started collecting books, stamps, or coins—all most respectable in the collecting world! Others collected dishes, tole trays, snuff boxes, and a thousand other things. But, wait—what about all those collections of lunch boxes, milk glass, comic books, or matchbooks? They certainly have a place too. Later in the century, the internet and companies like eBay opened up a whole world of collecting from your computer screen. No longer was it necessary to leave your home to hunt for treasures; you could sit in your pajamas and shop for anything you could possibly collect with the click of your mouse. This did make it easier to find what you were seeking, but it also sometimes revealed that what you thought was rare was actually quite available or maybe downright common. The internet also leveled the pricing, to some extent, since people could easily compare what similar pieces were going for. Suddenly, you could shop the world instead of just your local antique store or mall. (Personally, I still love to comb the flea markets and antique stores for my collectibles. The thrill of the hunt and the stories that go along with it are just not the same when shopping on the computer.)

The twenty-first century has brought us even faster and more efficient search engines that make it even easier to find the rare and unusual collectibles. We now have the world at our shopping fingertips; we can easily research and find the things we enjoy and love to collect. Online auctions make it easy to bid on items in any city or country. (Of course, we are now also bidding against people from those other cities and countries.) I remember going to auctions on rainy, cold nights when few people turned out and scoring some real treasures at great prices. Whether people are shopping at their computer screens or scouring their favorite antique shops or flea markets, they can and will collect just about anything and everything. Maybe they shouldn't—but they can!

In my opinion, everyone should collect something. It's very educational besides being a lot of fun. I'm always learning something from fellow collectors. The best stories are always told by collectors, and then you also become a collector of great stories, along with the artifacts.

A Passion for Collecting

Many years ago a dear friend that I went to college with started collecting miniature books. I don't think I even knew what a miniature book was. I had seen some very tiny books of the works of Shakespeare and a tiny prayer book that had belonged to my great-grandmother, but it didn't register that these were in fact "miniature" books. (Little did I know that there are very serious guidelines about what will or will not qualify as miniature.) He was very picky about the sizes he would consider, as well as the subjects and authors he was interested in. (He confessed to me that the works of Shakespeare were common in the small book world, even though he had several.) After he had accumulated quite a collection, maybe seventy-five or eighty, he discovered a fabulous old pagoda-like structure, about the size of a dollhouse, which was painted Chinese red with gold accents. Having a good eye for display, he arranged the miniature books in this charming red pagoda. I couldn't believe how interesting they all looked—tiny books stacked and arranged on their sides or leaning against each other, some open and some closed, some on top of tiny little boxes, and others on intricate carved stands. He also added a few odd little ivory statues, several ancient tattered and embroidered fabrics, and some beautiful polished rocks and minerals. It was amazing! I couldn't get over it! All these little books displayed together and lovingly arranged in one wonderful cabinet became my first look at a cabinet of curiosities! I think that was when it dawned on me that if you put a number of similar objects together something magical can happen. One is nice, two is better, and three is a collection.

About the same time, I started to get interested in antiques and interior design and began to collect things I liked and could possibly afford. I loved small sterling silver cigarette holders (I used to fill them with cigarettes—for looks only!) and small silver tabletop pieces such as pierced bowls and trumpet vases. Soon my interests expanded to silhouettes, Italian marble stone fruit, parian busts, tole trays, Chinese mudmen, blue-and-white Chinese export porcelain, ceramic glove molds (because they are so weird, they make me laugh every time I see one), antique pocket watch holders, antique books, basalt ware and my all-time favorite—a nineteenth-century ironstone transferware in a pattern called Etruscan Vases. When I found the first piece, I thought I had the only one in the world. (Was I ever wrong!) One piece turned into one hundred and the chase and the fun began. It has been a passion and a hobby and a profession all put together and I have loved each and every minute of the hunt!

Not only did I enjoy searching for more collections, I loved decorating my home with the collections and displaying them for my own enjoyment. Ugly walls and lots of bad wallpaper were hidden in my first apartment behind a collection of tole trays and silhouettes. Arrangements of transferware plates decorated the walls of my dining room when I had very little artwork. (I had more plates on the wall than in the pantry!) Tabletops were covered in collections of whatever I was interested in at the time, oftentimes making it difficult for a guest to set a drink down. The decorating and the collecting worked well together, and it was an easy way to personalize and furnish my rooms with the things I loved to collect. (After all, liking your own stuff should be what really matters.)

As time passed and I moved from apartment to condo to house, some collections worked better than others, and it was necessary to edit and sell things I didn't love as much and start a search for something new. Learning to edit is an important part of collecting. It can be hard to do but it will make for a finer collection. (I still have a long way to go in this department.) Things you are no longer as fond of can be just what another collector is looking for. So edit and sell and upgrade your collections and spread the love around!

Collecting on a Higher Level

Which brings us to my current home, a high-rise I share with another collector who is as opinionated as me and who likes "stuff" as much as I do. Most high-rise apartments, or condos, are really nothing but bland boxes with, hopefully, lots of glass and if you are really lucky, a view. In this case I lucked out with a whole wall of glass and a wonderful view of downtown Dallas. When we bought, the rooms themselves didn't have a lot of architectural interest. With its heavily textured walls, orange doors, and lots of arches, the space was somewhat reminiscent of an Italian or maybe a Mexican restaurant. It hadn't been updated since the '80s and it was in need of a complete gut and redo. In our redesign, we closed off or resized doorways and eliminated all the arched openings. We smoothed or papered the walls and replaced the interior doors and moldings with a better scale. A major decision had to do with the flooring. I finally decided on a wood herringbone pattern with borders to cover the concrete floor. The result? The floors are the focal point of the rooms and most are left bare. The walls are painted a warm neutral color (they sometimes look mocha and sometimes a little more yellow depending on the time of day) and the curtains match the walls. All in all, I wanted a clean neutral background to assemble our furniture and artwork and most of my collections.

Most of my favorite things have a home now. The walls of the master bedroom are covered with primarily nineteenth-century watercolors, away from direct sunlight. Silhouettes and basalt busts also adorn the walls of the bedroom—with parian busts here and there. My favorite piece of bedroom furniture is an old fold-down secretary desk that belonged to my grandmother and was faux-grained years ago to resemble bird's-eye maple with ebony inlay. It has always had a place of honor in my residences and is now filled to the max with Chinese export porcelains (many from the Hatcher Collection of shipwrecked Ming Dynasty porcelains) and an ever-growing collection of mudmen.

The Etruscan Vases transferware is housed in a mahogany cabinet in the dining room, along with a collection of stone fruit and nineteenth-century neoclassical vases and parian busts. First edition books, more parian ware, art books, family photos, and my collection of pocket watches sit on a series of stands that decorate the library and give me joy every day when I look at them. The condo is no longer bland, and there are no more empty walls to fill. My new rule is this: one new treasure in and one old treasure out, except for stone fruit or mudmen. They really don't take up much space and I can always squeeze in another one. (Spoken like a true collector.)

FACING: The entry hall accessories get changed often, depending on the latest collection! I do love this set of three Aesthetic movement vases with Greek key borders displayed on a gilt-edged mirror plateau in front of artwork by Victor Vasarely (a little old, a little new). The candlesticks are early 19th-century French.

ABOVE: The dining table holds not only books but a varied collection of parian ware, Regency candelabras, and a pair of antique French bronze and marble tazzas. The porcelain incense burners are copies of antique ones. Skirted tables help when the room gets too "leggy" and provide a lot of hidden storage.

The larger living room seating area displays a collection of 20th-century artwork by Miro, Vasarely and Graham Sutherland with an eclectic mix of traditional and modern furnishings. I think the grouping of artwork over the sofa is more fun than just a single painting would be.

My grandmother's old secretary was painted in a faux bois bird's-eye maple and holds a collection of Chinese export porcelain and, of course, mudmen. I love having it in the bedroom because it's the first thing I see when I open my eyes in the morning.

FACING: An ebonized French desk holds a collection of antique books, obelisks of marble and rock crystal and a Victorian wax bust. This desk has a red leather top, which is a lovely background color for almost anything you set on the surface.

TOP: One of two American games tables in the dining room displays part of the collection of Etruscan Vases ironstone transferware from England.

BOTTOM: A 19th-century Empire-style sideboard holds a collection of parian busts and vintage marble fruit, all beneath a wall grouping of artwork by Pat Steir, Victor Vasarely and Henry Moore. The bronze candlesticks are called grotesques, and I wish I could find a few more!

Bedroom walls papered in a very subtle yellow-and-gold Osborne & Little pattern are hung with a collection of 19th-century watercolors and silhouettes. The variety of shapes and sizes and the use of pairs framing the headboard gives the wall added interest.

"Collecting is a form of learning"

A carved wooden lamb (originally part of a Christmas crèche) gazes at a ceramic pear sculpture on the piano, while an antique carved wooden Chinese acrobat balances a porcelain vase.

An antique French bookcase holds more of the 150-plus pieces of Etruscan Vases dinnerware sets, and neoclassical 19th-century vases and classical parian ware busts adorn the top. I liked that the piece is low enough in height to allow display on top.

A Lake House Full of Collections
and Family Keepsakes

Over a decade ago, I rather magically acquired a lake house in the Ozark Mountains just outside of Eureka Springs. I wasn't really looking for a second home, but since I had talked about it with my sister, she would occasionally drive around the lake looking at property and then send me photos of houses for sale.

One day she sent me a link to a listing that had all of my requirements—the most important being a screened porch with a lake view. I really don't like to be on the water or have to deal with boats and boat docks. Launching a boat or caring for it, or dealing with the spiders and critters that always seem to be found in an unused boat, is really not my thing. However, I do love to look at the water—especially from a bug-free screened porch. (I guess you get the idea that I do not like bugs!) And I really didn't care about the rest of the house that came with the porch, as long as there were several bathrooms and enough bedrooms for a few occasional houseguests. I had never had a second home before and the crazy idea seemed a bit scary. I decided to just ride this out and see if it would really come to pass.

Amazingly, everything fell into place quite easily and I found myself the owner of a sunny little lake house with no particular architectural style—probably from the late '70s or early '80s. It was cosmetically dated but not in terrible shape—livable, but not lovable. Making it my own became a slow, weekend fix-up project with my family and friends. We laughed and partied and painted and slept late on the newly arrived mattresses (usually the first thing you run out and buy)—and carried in the odd tables and lamps, etc. Relatives and friends always want to give you their castoffs for a lake house. I constantly had to turn down old mattresses, furniture, and lamps.

I first thought I would go in a different design direction from my home in Dallas; however, I realized my favorite room in Dallas was the garden room, with its slipcovered furniture and mixture of inherited Victorian antiques and tole trays, plates, and silhouettes. Also, it was all upholstered in what is apparently my favorite color combination—red and green! Why not send all that to the lake and redo the garden room in Dallas? It was a great plan and everything fit perfectly in the new lake house. (However, my plans to redo the old garden room in a new look failed. I simply replaced the furniture with almost identical pieces, all in the same colors—red and green!)

Because of the house's lack of architectural style, I decided to focus on decorating with collections of things I loved and furniture I had inherited and that held sweet memories of their previous owner—whether relative or friend. (Only good memories would let the piece qualify—no bad karma here!) The walls were soon covered with tole trays, watercolors from estate sales and local art galleries, silhouettes, old ancestral portraits and vintage oil paintings, colorful plates, and family photos. Almost everything had a story or a memory behind it, including my multilayered, slipcovered sofa from my first apartment, the antique cherry cupboard from a dear deceased friend, the painting of a local mountain bluff that always hung behind the easy chair where Grandmother Marrs sat and read, the furniture my mom helped me spray paint for the porch, and the grass shades my dad and I spent the day hanging on the windows. (Dad died only a few years later and I am so thankful for all the lake visits we shared.) The lamps in the living room were ordered from a catalog and came in more pink than red, so Mom got out her oil paints and we repainted the clothing of the Chinese people on the lamps to work better in the living room. We laughed at ourselves for doing it but loved the results. Such fun we had, and now when I visit, I often think about all those happy times when I look around the rooms. I remember being so proud of and loving everything that came into the house and was hung on the wall or placed on a tabletop.

I know it isn't fancy or expensive or the current design trend, but I feel so good each time I visit or spend the weekend there surrounded by all my humble inherited and found treasures. I wouldn't trade a single moment or a single memory that was created during the decorating of the house. Yes, it could be more up-to-date with what is trendy or cool in the design world—sometimes I'm almost embarrassed it is so humble. I don't have a polished-chrome sputnik chandelier, multicolored abstract shag area rug, abstract painting, granite countertop, white subway tile bathroom, or upholstered headboard. Everything is pretty much secondhand or slightly redone, and there's lots and lots of brown furniture—all with a story proudly behind it.

A guest room furnished with a pair of inherited antique spindle beds and an American Empire games table gets freshened up with an updated toile fabric in chartreuse and chocolate brown. The painting is a midcentury oil and the ceramic pineapple was bought in Mexico.

I think one good-looking fabric, like this cotton print, used on everything can unify a room full of many different furniture pieces. The inherited glass-front cupboard holds a cherished collection of Flow Blue dishes. The oil painting of a local mountain road belonged to my grandmother.

TOP: I never met a chair I didn't like, as you can tell from the living room. Occasional tables and an antique cherry bookcase, along with a collection of hooked rugs, antique paintings and local watercolors decorate the room. Everything gets a slipcover in the same fabric used in the dining room.

BOTTOM: A somewhat somber ancestral portrait dominates the living room, which is adorned with antique chairs, an old family ironstone pitcher, and a collection of silhouettes painted on glass.

FACING: A screened porch is a big part of life at the lake. The terra-cotta monkey always makes me laugh as it swings over a table set for lunch with vintage glasses and lettuce leaf plates.

ABOVE: The master bedroom is always a happy room, with its red walls and collection of circus posters. The bedside tables were once the ends of a large dining room table.

Many times I meet new clients and find out they are collectors. Sometimes they tell me and sometimes I discover it on visiting their home. I'm always fascinated or intrigued by what they collect. It may be very obvious upon entering the house and seeing walls or cabinets filled with their assortment. Other times, as I look around a home, I see similar items scattered all over the house, and sometimes the owners don't even realize that they have accrued quite a number of related pieces of art. That's okay with me—I enjoy seeing what treasures they have and thinking of a plan to organize it and make it more attractive in their home.

The clients who are serious collectors usually want help in adding more display space for their collections (hence the collector's malady mentioned earlier). Sometimes they are planning an expansion of the house for more collections. Often I am involved in designing custom display cabinets or lining the backs of existing cases with new fabric or working on better lighting. Many collectibles need special bases or stands to be displayed properly, and each time a new one arrives it must be measured and its placement discussed.

The clients who really haven't realized they have a collection just need a little encouragement in that department. I usually mention just how many similar items they have all over the house and wouldn't it be interesting if we gathered them all up and possibly placed them in a large cabinet or a single bookcase. (I'm amazed at how much credit I get for this simple observation.)

Over the years I have seen the most wonderful collections that clients have put together of antique silver, art glass, Imari, silhouettes, and designer handbags, to name a few. I have arranged them on the walls, in antique cabinets, and in lighted bookcases and custom display vitrines. Sometimes I just rearrange shelves that are already pretty darn nice, in hopes of showing off the collection in a slightly different way. This is especially exciting when the client moves into a different home. We are creatures of habit, and a lot of times clients want to arrange everything in almost exactly the same way they had it for years. I encourage (and sometimes beg) them to let me try something different with the arrangement or placement of the artwork or special collections. By arranging the artwork in a different way or by moving things around a little, I can give the client a whole new appreciation for the collection. Every time I change things up a bit I hear my clients comment that they now love a painting or sculpture that they never appreciated before. Sometimes you just need a fresh eye to see things differently!

It is always so interesting to me to see all the different things people collect or are drawn to. One client likes porcelains, another photography, and yet another antique paintings. I love all these special collections assembled by my clients who obviously enjoyed the hunt for their treasures. Most have a story about each piece—the trip they were on when they found it or the auction item that got away. I certainly enjoy listening!

"Display your collection in one cabinet
or on one wall for the greatest effect."

Victorian Silver

Victorian silver, or for that matter, most antique silver is really lovely. The crafts-manship alone is remarkable, even if you don't like the style, surely you can appre-ciate that. I'm amazed at the people who cannot appreciate it but only worry about having to polish it. (Let's not even go there.) What's even better with this collection is that you can actually use a lot of it—to set a beautiful table or sideboard, for example. This client really does love silver and is so passionate about her collection. We have just about filled every nook and cabinet she has—and she is still on the hunt! Her dining room is always full of wonderful pieces, and I know it makes her happy! To keep everything from getting too serious with all the mahogany furni-ture, we had an artist paint the dining room walls a rather whimsical floral design in her favorite colors.

FACING: A mahogany curved-front corner cabinet holds a collection of Victorian silver child's cups and antique Limoges plates, topped off with silver chalices and a horse show trophy. Note the unique design of the glass door.

ABOVE LEFT: Who doesn't like champagne—especially served on this gorgeous rosewood games table? Even the peacock seems happy.

ABOVE RIGHT: The handsome chest between two dining room windows holds an early 19th-century samovar.

ABOVE: The magnificent mahogany breakfront with beautifully shaped interior shelves holds the owner's collection of unique silver table service pieces, including wonderful teapots and ornate trays.

FACING: An early 19th-century gilt convex mirror from New Orleans hangs over a sideboard set for tea with a gorgeous silver tea service, graceful Edwardian five-light candelabras and an assortment of silver serving pieces.

"Display your collections in rooms you love and use."

FACING: The rosewood pedestal card table at the end of the hallway looks out onto the garden. It serves as a place for card games or as an extra dining table. Encircling a lovely silver epergne are several examples of the owner's large collection of Victorian silver bride's baskets.

ABOVE: Two beautiful bride's baskets show the elaborate borders, lovely shapes and intricate handle details.

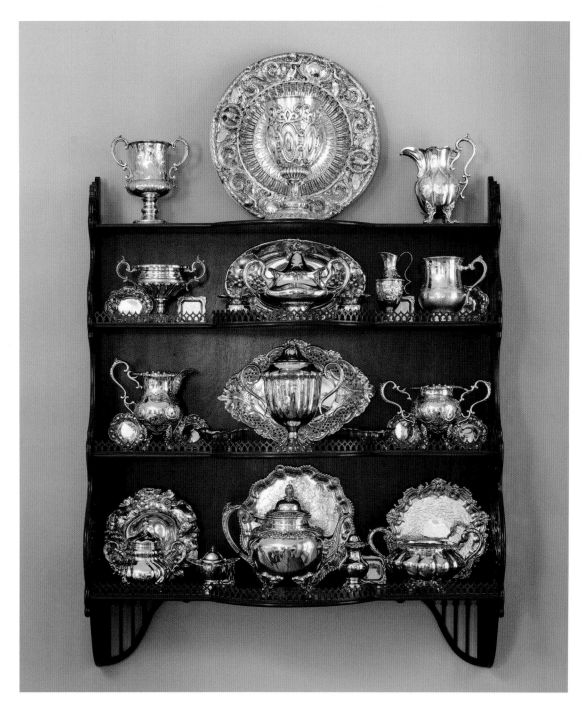

ABOVE: Another effective display piece is the wall shelf. This intricately carved mahogany one with a full wooden back shows off a collection of Victorian nut dishes and small pitchers. The shelves help to organize this collection of smalls, and the silver pieces really stand out against the rich wood.

FACING: I would put a corner cabinet in every room if I could. This lovely old pine piece is filled to the brim with teapots, trays and biscuit barrels. The shaped shelves are perfect for display.

Art Glass

Art glass can also be decorative as well as useful. Hang it on the wall or put it on a pedestal or fill it with flowers—what's not to love about collecting this unique art form. This client has had a grand time traveling all over the world and bringing home piece after piece of beautiful art glass. (I'm amazed that they have all arrived unscathed.) We had to make sure that this house was bright and light-filled to show off all her favorite pieces.

FACING: Notice how the painting plays off the design on the art glass sitting on this games table. Even the chair fabric becomes a big part of the color composition. We freshened up the old brown game chairs with a coat of white paint.

ABOVE: A glass-front and mirror-back display cabinet shows off some larger pieces of art glass along with family photos and books. The mirror back lets you enjoy all sides of the glass pieces.

ABOVE: A dramatic chest and mirror fill one of the smaller dining room walls and reflect the light from the window as well as the colorful art glass. In this case, the mirror is about as pretty as what it reflects.

FACING: The art glass hung on the wall and placed on the console table inspired the warm, colorful design of the dining room. We painted the walls white and changed the wood floors out to stone. It's a perfect place to dine and enjoy the artwork as well as the glass collection. Who needs a rug or curtains when you have all this to take in?

Silhouettes

Silhouettes, or cutouts, are a favorite collectible of mine. But I was left in the dust by this collection my client put together. She has the big names and some great examples. I remember having my silhouette done as a little boy—which I still have. I even have a current silhouette, although I don't care for all the chins they added. Anyway, I love silhouettes, especially in their original wooden frames. They look so lovely arranged in groupings on a wall—especially in this library on this particularly pretty shade of blue.

FACING: This comfy corner of a library showcases a very special collection of silhouettes by some of the most famous names. I really like the soft blue wall color with all the wooden frames. The exquisite damask on the exposed wood armchair is by Scalamandré.

ABOVE: The silhouette of the two children is by Edouart (1789–1861), and the charming little girl above is by H. A. Frith of the Royal Victoria Gallery (after 1837–c. 1854).

FACING: It's never too late to have your silhouette done. Here I am hanging proudly with these other gentlemen on a wall in the bedroom. I also have the one my mother had done of me when I was a child.

ABOVE: A charming primitive corner cabinet in the morning room shows off its owner's collection of blue and white dishes and American sandwich and flint glass. The silhouette of a child on the left was done by Frederick Frith (1846) and the one on the right is by Edouart (1843).

Orange Fitzhugh

Orange Fitzhugh is a beautiful color and pattern of Chinese export porcelain. I was so very lucky to get to build two wonderful corner cabinets for this lovely set. The shell design and curved shelves worked perfectly to house this special collection that was lovingly put together by a very discerning collector.

FACING: So many interesting shapes are seen in this collection of orange Fitzhugh, including lots of pairs. We painted the back of the cabinet a soft golden beige to accent but not overpower the porcelains.

ABOVE: My client loves arranging flowers as well as collecting—and she is very good at both. More orange Fitzhugh is seen throughout her lovely dining room, and her floral creation is reflected in the polished wood table. A classic Fortuny fabric covers the dining room chairs.

Antique Paintings

I have a longtime client who loves to entertain and I always make sure she has a beautiful dining room. She is a perfect hostess who sets an exquisite table and always has the most charming guests. (Sometimes she even includes me.) Her late husband had put together quite a collection of antique paintings during his travels over the years. We decided to display them salon-style in the dining room for guests to enjoy during dinner. Soft lighting—the glow from the red ceiling—and lots of flickering candles create a special room for this collection.

FACING: Antique kitten oil paintings, collected by my client's late husband, are a favorite from this grouping of Victorian artwork on the fireplace wall of her dining room.

ABOVE: The portrait of the lady in purple has been a focal point in all of her homes. Warm white walls and an elegant red ceiling create a perfect backdrop for this wonderful hostess, who loves to entertain and does it so beautifully.

OVERLEAF: I gathered up most of the antique paintings from throughout the house and rehung them salon style in the dining room for everyone to enjoy during frequent dinner parties. We actually transformed the original living room into the dining room to accommodate her large table and many chairs, and now a roaring fire can be enjoyed during dinner.

Parian Ware

Parian ware, a type of biscuit porcelain, was the poor man's marble and was widely collected during the nineteenth century. Almost every important person was captured in parian, along with all the Greek and Roman mythology characters. Most people have no idea what it is or probably never gave it a thought—except for a few of us who find it really beautiful. I love the way the creamy white, smooth texture looks against certain warm colors like apricot and butter yellow. You can collect to your heart's content because there is a lot of it out there. I prefer the classical busts but I've picked up pitchers and vases too. It's fun to add them to your dining table and mix in with fresh flowers.

FACING: This breakfront, with its richly painted interior, was the perfect backdrop for my collection of various parian busts and figurines. I even added an antique gold braid to the front edge of each shelf.

ABOVE: This large parian ware piece depicting Homer was found on a trip to Ireland and was carefully bundled and brought home in the airplane's overhead compartment. He sits proudly on the top shelf in the library in the center of a collection of busts.

FACING: The dining room of a house I formerly owned had "butta" yellow walls. I miss the collection of antique hot air balloon prints that hung there. Why did I ever sell them? I always have a tinge of regret about selling anything.

ABOVE: Parian busts look good in front of a collection of antique first-edition books also in the library. I mixed in antique pocket watches displayed on a collection of pocket watch holders. The woman in blue opening a letter (artist unknown) is one of my favorites. She looks frozen in time. I often wonder if it was good news or bad—we will never know.

OVERLEAF: One of the walls of books in our library also features a lot of family photos. But it *is* a library, and books *do* make a room beautiful to me. One could actually read them too. I so enjoy my top shelf of parian ware busts and figures. So many trips and so much fun shopping—that's a big part of the joy of collecting!

Churchill Memorabilia

I love clients that come to me with a dream of something they really want in a room. A contractor brought me in on this project and I am so glad he did! It was for a couple who owned a lovely historical home; however, what I was asked to work on was the quarters above the garage. The husband is an attorney and has had a lifetime fascination with Winston Churchill and especially Churchill's country home, Chartwell. He wanted his new home office above the garage to be reminiscent of Churchill's study at Chartwell. My first thought was that the space was too small and too different from the original; I could hardly imagine the possibility. However, after thinking about it and studying the interiors and the finishes of the actual Chartwell study, I thought we could somehow capture the feel of the space, although on a much smaller scale.

We began by opening up the ceilings to the maximum height and adding old wooden beams in the style of the Chartwell study. The floors were stained in a similar light color, the walls were done in plaster, and several recessed stained wood bookcases (ala Chartwell) were built to accommodate the client's law books. He wanted a bar in the space—since old Winston could put away a few—so we created a large antique-looking cabinet that concealed an ice maker and refrigerator and would serve as a bar. Leather lounge chairs, a writing desk, and various antique oriental rugs completed the rather manly Churchillian (I made that up) office. We hung the client's collection of Churchill photographs up the stairway and added a few antique paintings and small collections, such as the mudmen on the mantel of the fireplace. I think Churchill might have felt right at home—the client claims he sometimes smells cigar smoke.

"A collection is a window
into the mind of the collector."

FACING: On the staircase wall up to the office is a collection of black-and-white photographs having to do with Churchill. I think my client enjoys climbing those stairs and savoring each photo again. The wooden ceiling and trim and the plaster walls are reminiscent of Chartwell.

ABOVE: We actually designed a piece of furniture that looked antique but that housed a refrigerator and could be used as a bar cabinet. I am so lucky to work with wonderful craftspeople who can build and install such beautiful pieces.

ABOVE: A collection of antique law books and a fireplace in the style of Chartwell are all beneath a beautiful ceiling of antique beams. Leather reading chairs, antique oriental carpets and a rare student lamp complete the room, which the client uses as a home office.

FACING: The client found this very interesting painting for over the fireplace, and I added the collection of mudmen on the mantel shelf. They seem right at home—I'm sure Churchill would approve.

Imari Porcelains

The greatest compliment is when a fellow designer asks you to help with her home. In this case she was also a great collector of Imari. She actually introduced me to mudmen too—but that is another story. She and her husband had traveled all over but had especially loved England, and they had brought back many lovely pieces of Imari over the years. When they decided to move to a townhouse I was lucky enough to get to help plan the new rooms. We had so much fun arranging and hanging their much-loved collection of nineteenth-century British art, mudmen, English Silver, papier-mâché, hurricane globes, and especially the vast amounts of Imari. We arranged the Imari in the entry, the dining room, the Welch cupboard in the living room, and even over the bed in the master bedroom. I always thought it unified the design of the house and, of course, it looked different in each room. How can you have too much Imari? (Impossible.)

FACING: An antique Welch cupboard from around 1870 holds a vast collection of Imari plates and vases, inkwells and spill vases collected by the owner on many trips abroad over the years.

ABOVE: A lovely inherited Imari bowl is used as a centerpiece, surrounded by a collection of antique English silver candlesticks. The wall covering is Bailey & Griffin.

A five-piece Imari mantel garniture graces the top of the fireplace. The mantel, originally painted white, was faux grained to imitate burled walnut. Wing chair fabric and curtain fabric are by F. Schumacher.

Papier-mâché wall brackets, trays and letter boxes are hung around a fine old English mirror. The pair of Imari vases are actually tea caddies. An exquisite Imari charger and a pair of lovely vases sit on the entry lowboy.

FACING: A set of four oriental watercolors accent the fabric bed crown. Imari bedside lamps light the bed dressed in Hamburg House linens. The bedroom fabrics are by Brunschwig & Fils and Bailey and Griffin.

ABOVE: Nineteenth-century Imari chargers are hung next to a very old American dresser and mirror inherited from the owner's great-grandparents. On the wall at the end of the hall is a very rare pair of Imari car vases— made for the inside of an automobile to add fragrance and a touch of elegance. I so wish that car accessory had never gone out of style!

OVERLEAF: This delightful living room is where the owners entertain and enjoy all the beautiful things they have collected over the years. The lighted display cabinet holds a collection of porcelains, and a charming oil of the English countryside hangs over the mantel.

Photography and Handbags

A lot of women have a passion for handbags, but few enjoy collecting them as much as this client! Lovely to look at and even more lovely to carry—these babies are really works of art! The quality and materials are extraordinary, and I loved getting to arrange and organized them by color and size. Can you blame me? She also has a thing for shoes—are you surprised? I can see them all in a museum one day!

Originally, the house had mostly antique furniture pieces, but we decided to add photography—especially black-and-white pieces to contrast with the dark wood furniture and give the rooms a fresh look. Red walls, which the client loves, are also a perfect background for the growing collection of fashion photographs.

FACING: Black-and-white photographs of Hollywood royalty are hung over a bedside chest. A full color range of Hermes bags are cataloged before being placed in special storage or display cabinets.

ABOVE: An acrylic wall shelf in the owner's dressing area holds a collection of Louboutin and Yves Saint Laurent clutches.

FACING: F. Schumacher's crimson faux-crocodile wall covering lines the walls and ceiling of this glamorous sitting area. A Daum crystal tulip vase sits on the mirrored chest.

ABOVE: An antique armoire was repurposed as storage and display for part of the owner's collection of Hermes bags.

ABOVE: A photograph by Tyler Shields titled *Chanel Legs* hangs over a French armchair covered in leopard-print fabric. The red bag is Chanel.

FACING: Helmut Newton photos *Dressed and Naked* complete a study in black and white over the piano.

Chinese Mudmen

When the farmers in China, ca. 1880 and forward, were through planting their crops, they would often spend time making small mud figurines to sell for extra money. Formed by hand out of the local clay, the figurines were of men, women (these are very rare), wise men, and sages. The hands and faces were not painted or glazed and were left in the natural color of the mud. (Some are almost lily white and others are very dark, depending on the mud and the location in China where the mud was dug up.) My parents were given one by an elderly lady who had obviously traveled to China. I (the appointed keeper of everything in my family) kept the little Confucius-looking guy (since I didn't know what it was) for years and one day a collector friend informed me it was a mudman. To my surprise, I had a very old mudman and I soon was on a quest to get him as many friends as I could find. They are somewhat plentiful and aren't always expensive, so I decided to be picky and not purchase any with obvious damage, such as missing fingers or toes. I loved the colors of their robes and the expressions on their faces, but I became obsessed with the bald ones with topknots. Why, I don't know, but I was crazy about those and couldn't find enough of them. I met a new client who was about as crazy over mudmen as I was, and we talked mudmen and compared notes and shopped competitively—but nicely! When we worked on her new house, we were determined to have a special place for the mudmen, and we did! I love the way she arranges hers!

FACING: A client who collects mudmen uses a unique carved stand to display her favorites. I covet her little golden bridge out in front, but she will not sell it to me!

ABOVE: My client arranged these mudmen on her bedroom fireplace mantel. I love the simple, asymmetrical arrangement beneath this beautiful painting by Sonia Grineva.

OVERLEAF: We designed this client's media room to have built-in shelves filled with mudmen on either side of the entertainment center so she can watch a movie and enjoy her collections at the same time. An antique leather trunk serves as a useful table in front of the custom sectional. The stunning painting is by Santa Fe artist Evelyne Boren.

"Edit your collection at least once a year."

I added an instant collection of mudmen when I was accessorizing this client's bookcase. Shame on me! The antique box was perfect to arrange them inside and on top.

FACING: The media room custom shelving on the right side of the television holds mudmen, a collection of bronzes and a pair of porcelain vases. The client has a great eye and is always rearranging, editing and adding to her collections. We still compete for the best mudmen and sometimes she lets me win.

III

Building a New Home
for a Collection

Sometimes housing a collection is more than just arranging a cabinet or building a room for it. Often it can involve building an entire house. I don't mean that each and every room in the residence houses a collection. (You could, I suppose, but that might be a little too much.) Usually, only the major rooms contain the collections. Frequently, the collection influences the design of the house, and the focus of the major rooms is to display a collection or several collections.

"Collect what you love and want to live
with for a while rather than what is collectible
'of the moment.'"

Inherited Furniture and Collectibles

Years ago a very dear client called to tell me she and her family were going to build a new house. I had helped her for several years with her present home and we were always on the same wavelength. Her grandfather, a cabinetmaker, had built her a dining table and set of chairs along with a buffet and a corner cabinet. They were all quite handsome, traditional furniture pieces in the style of Hepplewhite and they meant a great deal to her. (I loved them the first time I saw them, which pleased her since the first decorator she interviewed suggested she get rid of them all.) She also had several inherited antique pieces, including chests and small tables, along with a lot of accessories, such as a collection of Blue Willow from her grandmother. (More about the Blue Willow later.)

After several conversations about how her family liked to live in their home and her basic requirements for numbers of bedrooms, bathrooms, etc., we started laying out the room arrangements. Since she had all this wonderful dining room furniture, we agreed on a large dining room with floor and wall space for all the pieces her grandfather had built. The walls were papered in a wonderful raspberry-colored moiré stripe, and the curtains are a classic, hand-blocked linen tree-of-life pattern. The corner cabinet held a collection of inherited English porcelain.

She didn't really want a formal living room so we decided, instead, to have a large entry hall with a fireplace nook the architect referred to as an inglenook. The entry was spacious enough for a large center table and seating not only in the inglenook but along other walls. The space was two stories in height, with a lovely staircase and the recessed fireplace inglenook adding architectural interest. The walls were paneled and painted a couple of shades of white and the upper level windows let in enormous amounts of natural light. The floors were wood and we stenciled a black checkerboard pattern over them. The entry could be intimate enough for two people to sit by the fire or large enough to accommodate lots of guests arriving for a party. I found a wonderful French settee in New Orleans which anchored one wall and allowed for additional seating. An antique tall case clock was also given a place of honor opposite the fireplace. We added a couple of ancestral portraits—purchased at an antique store (so they were someone else's ancestors)—which we thought was funny because guests always want to know if they are her ancestors. You can always pass them off as yours or tell the truth—either way you usually get a shocked look! I am amazed at the people who will not consider an antique portrait—even if it is exceptionally fine—because they are not related to the subject. Who's to know? If the people in the portraits are good-looking, it's a perfect opportunity to upgrade your relatives!

Another interesting thing happened during the building of the house. The small cottage that we replaced with the new house was brick. Out of the blue, several people inquired about the bricks that we removed and stacked and if they were for sale. The original house had been painted and didn't look that interesting; however, because of the flurry of interest, my client did some research and found out the bricks had been handmade for a much older demolished downtown Dallas building, and then repurposed for the cottage. With that background, no way were we getting rid of them! We used them for the flooring of the family room, kitchen, and breakfast room. Once the bricks were turned over, stained, and sealed, the floors were absolutely beautiful—nothing like what they had looked like on the former house. It gave the house a big dose of character, plus made for a great story!

One last funny thing had to do with the Blue Willow dishes my client inherited from her grandmother. Some were really old and fine; others were not so fine. She had paid everywhere from twenty-five cents to twenty-five dollars for the plates over the years. She used them to teach her granddaughters and little neighborhood girls about China when they came to her house for tea parties, and she often explained the story of the young lovers depicted on the dishes. When my client was quite young, elaborate tea parties had been staged with the Blue Willow dishes, kimonos (I know, I know, kimonos are Japanese and Blue Willow was developed in England), brightly colored umbrellas, and Chinese music blaring from the hi-fi! Every time she looks at the collection she smiles, remembering all those happy tea parties when she was a little girl. We found a lovely antique Welch cupboard to display them in the breakfast room so she can enjoy them every time she walks by.

For almost twenty years the decorating has remained pretty much the same except for freshening up the fabrics and replacing some of the case pieces with finer ones. We tweak the pillows and redecorate other rooms and update the kitchen and baths, but the entry and dining room remain pretty much the same. I am so proud of that, and I think it looks just as lovely as when it was first done. Lots of collections have been added—especially artwork from all of their travels. So each painting is, in itself, a story and a memory of a vacation or an event. I always loved meeting up with them after their return from a trip and talking about where to hang a new piece of artwork or what kind of frame it needed. Good houses, like collections, are always growing and changing and are never truly finished!

A mahogany corner cabinet, built by the client's grandfather, holds an English tea set in Imari colors, purchased in New Orleans.

The dining room curtains are a hand-blocked
linen print, with sun shades by Conrad
underneath. I use them a lot because I love
the way they filter the sunlight. The mirror
is antique and the tureen was found in
France. The wall covering is from Fonthill.
We recently added the slipcovers to visually
soften the dining chairs.

FACING: The entrance hall has stenciled floors. A bronze eagle, originally from the top of a flag pole, commands the center table. The architect was Larry E. Boerder.

ABOVE: An antique French hall tree, with its original drip pan, was purchased for this exact spot and holds a collection of the owner's antique walking sticks.

INHERITED FURNITURE AND COLLECTIBLES · 103

Another view of the entrance hall shows a Directoire canapé purchased in New Orleans from the shop of Gerrie Bremermann. The antique tall case clock is also from New Orleans. Pillow fabric is by Vervain.

The family room walls are covered in artwork—some old and some new. The painting on the far right was done by the client's daughter, Sally Taylor, who is an artist. The leaning painting on the Italian empire commode is by California midcentury artist Joan Savo.

ABOVE: A lovely small drop-front desk, built by the client's grandfather, found a perfect home by the back stairs. More artwork, collected by the clients on their travels, is stacked and hung above.

FACING: The Welch dresser in the breakfast room holds the client's charming collection of Blue Willow from her very entertaining grandmother, as well as a lovely group of ironstone pitchers. The wall clock was a gift from her mother-in-law. The trellis-pattern wall covering is by F. Schumacher.

Minerals and Geodes

I had been working on a wonderful new house for a while and we were discussing the library with the husband. It was to be a rather grand room with walnut-paneled walls, inset with walnut burl, a beautiful coved ceiling and lots of what I thought were going to be bookcases. When I inquired if the client had a lot of books, he responded mischievously with a "heck no!" I kind of liked that, so I just played along, but finally asked just what he intended to put on all those shelves. "My mineral and geode collection, of course," he replied. Okay, now we were getting someplace. Well, little did I know about his collection and the quantity of it. Eventually all the before-mentioned items were measured and cataloged and the spacing of the shelves decided, along with what needed special mounting stands and bases (almost everything did). Then we discussed fabric for the backs of the shelves and the special lighting that was necessary for the shelves. (Now I was excited and I knew this was going to be good.) It was a challenge—those things are heavy! Some sat on the shelves but other larger ones were mounted to the wall. When the project was finished, I thought (and still think) it looks every bit as good as rows of books. We still call it the library, though!

We furnished the room with comfortable traditional upholstery and antiques and a custom cocktail table with a pure white onyx top. The lady of the house loves and appreciates beautiful fabrics and has quite a collection of antique textiles. We hung many on the walls, like a favorite that became the design inspiration for the master bedroom. She also loves beautiful stone and marble and the house has stunning inlay floors and exotic stone countertops.

Another favorite collection was in the client's home office. He had a marvelous collection of arrowheads collected by himself and his father and grandfather. We hung them all behind his desk opposite the fireplace. What a nice tribute to his dad and a great backdrop for his desk.

On the lower level we created a man cave with games tables and pool tables and televisions and a lot of rugged collections such as dinosaur bones (which sit on a custom table with dinosaur feet) and ancient fossils mounted on the walls. The room also holds some rather interesting items he has collected over the years: a handmade model of a locomotive engine and an old Wooton desk he had always wanted. The whole room is a modern-day cabinet of curiosities!

ABOVE: Detail of one of the large, wall-mounted ammonites—obviously a star of the collection. We used a soft linen fabric to upholster the wall behind it.

FACING: Each geode and mineral has its own unique, custom-made stand and each one is individually lighted. The large table in front of the sofa was custom built and fitted with a top of perfectly clear white onyx.

The vast living room has a fireplace at each end and two seating areas. Beyond is the stairwell with its magnificent walnut staircase. The architect for the home was Clay Nelson.

"Beautiful isn't a bad thing."

An antique table the client had seen was the inspiration for the custom-built center table. The floors are walnut and the chandeliers are by Minton-Spidell.

FACING: We found the perfect-size antique chest and mirror for the entrance hall at Nick Brock Antiques. The 18th-century French mirror is 90 inches tall. A large geode on an acrylic base is placed on the entry chest.

ABOVE: A custom powder room vanity cabinet holds a Sherle Wagner egg-and-dart stone vessel sink. A collection of antique butterfly prints hang on the walls. Note the unique stone details of the flooring.

ABOVE: The library offers a view to the side garden. An antique writing desk is placed behind the sofa; the two chairs are covered in F. Schumacher.

FACING: A lovely and very delicate antique textile covers a small stool. The lady of the house has a passion for beautiful antique embroidered fabrics.

FACING: Two antique cane-back wing chairs flank a stunning marble-top round table. The bar in the background has a very unusual stone top and splash with shaped sides. Note the wood transition from walnut to a lighter wood in the adjoining office.

ABOVE: The coved ceiling in Venetian plaster is highlighted by the antique chandelier from Embree & Lake Antiques. The library is an elegant but comfortable room with lots of beautiful collections to enjoy.

A peaceful sitting area in the master suite boasts a monumental stone fireplace. A wall-hung antique textile from Wolf Hall Antiques was the inspiration for the color scheme of the room.

The landing at the top of the main staircase features built-in shelving for handmade wooden vases and birds and niches for artwork. The library table, custom-built in walnut for this space, displays an intricate wooden art piece.

ABOVE: The husband's office has custom leather seating. Fabrics and finishes were chosen to keep the room light and to not compete with the view of the garden.

FACING: A wonderful collection of framed arrowheads is displayed behind the desk. The lighter-stained wall paneling contrasts with the dark walnut of the adjoining library. Colorful roman shades add a dash of color against neutral walls. The ornate chandelier is antique.

"Train your collector's eye by studying the best examples."

ABOVE: Designing special bases for the owner's collections—including this one with "dinosaur" feet—was great fun. Sometimes I think clients just want to see if we can really make their dreams a reality!

FACING: Another corner of the room shows fossils mounted on the wall as well as the monumental T-rex on the floor. The walls were upholstered in fabric to conceal holes from rehanging pieces as the collection grew and to contrast with all the walnut of the floors and trim.

FACING: This room doubles as a game room and a display room for various collections, such as this handmade wooden locomotive engine.

ABOVE: A magnificent Wooton desk, long admired by the owner, has a special place of honor.

French Antiques and Porcelains

Sometimes you get a dream job and you have to pinch yourself that it's real. This undertaking was that special! First, I had great clients who really had a clear vision of what they wanted and then we had a wonderful team that included the architect, builder, and me as interior designer. Projects like this don't come along that often and they also take a very long time. We were in the design process for a couple of years, and the construction of the house took about three years. However, it was a labor of love on everyone's part.

The house was in the French style, and the clients were busy during the construction traveling to Europe and purchasing antiques and artwork and collectibles for the interiors. They had a serious love of French furniture and decorative art pieces, especially porcelains. All the purchases were measured and cataloged as they were purchased and many rooms were built around those particular pieces. The marble pattern and the colors of the marble for the rotunda were inspired by the chapel at Versailles and we even built our own Hall of Mirrors. Carpets were woven for all of the major rooms and ornate plaster walls and ceilings were designed and installed. Each room became the perfect backdrop for the collection it contained. Although the house is quite formal, the clients enjoy living and entertaining in not only the grand entry rotunda but each unique room. The husband enjoys giving tours and sharing his love of French antiques and porcelains. From hosting chamber music to rock band concerts in the garden, this dream house has brought much joy to the owners and their lucky guests.

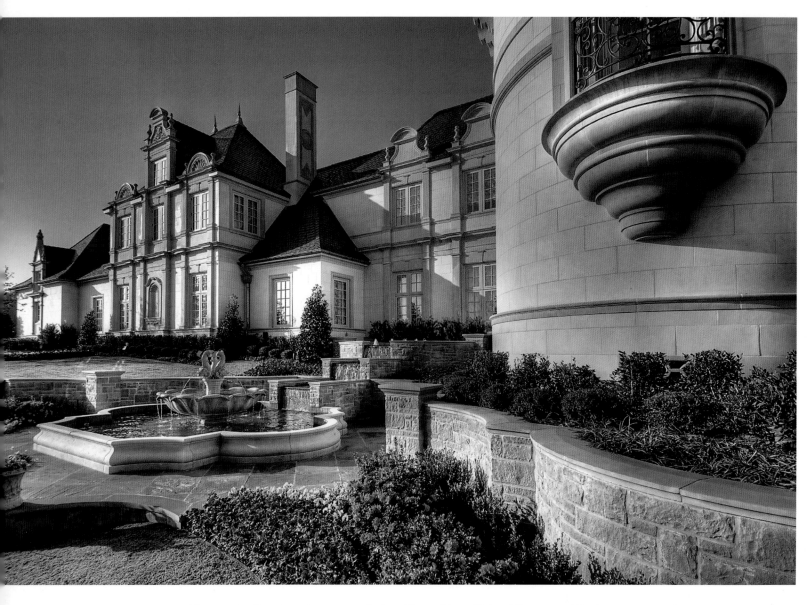

ABOVE: The massive limestone house was designed by architect Richard Drummond Davis.

FACING: The main staircase with beautifully detailed railing is adjacent to the rotunda. The large lantern is by Thomas Grant Chandeliers.

FACING: Light filters into the rotunda and onto a massive marble tazza. The design of the floors was inspired by the chapel at Versailles. Important collections of 17th- and 18th-century furniture and art pieces are displayed on the perimeter walls.

ABOVE: The pillars and intricate marble flooring pattern of the rotunda are even more spectacular when viewed from above.

The ornate plaster walls of the salon, just off the rotunda, are accented in gold leaf. The fabric for all the seating and wall upholstery is by Scalamandré. Many of the furniture pieces were acquired in Paris.

The Scalamandré upholstery on this wall of the salon is an elegant backdrop for the Louis XIV ormolu-mounted marquetry commode and a pair of Louis XVI inlaid ebony marquetry pedestals.

ABOVE: The "Hall of Mirrors," though somewhat smaller than the original, is highly decorative, with a painted ceiling and elaborate marble flooring. The neoclassic-style, ormolu-mounted, ebonized pedestals are 19th century, and the secretaire at the end of the hallway is Louis XVI. The wall of exterior windows reflects light onto the mirrors placed directly opposite, just like the original.

FACING: The dining room features a custom table with a magnificent Empire ormolu centerpiece. All fabric is Brunschwig & Fils silk damask. The signed bronze chandelier is antique.

WTX.COM

The high ceilings of the attic space called for elaborate beam craftsmanship. It became the "Gothic" room, where a collection of Gothic-inspired 19th-century bronzes are displayed. Many a musical evening has taken place here. An elegant bar helps to liven up even the shyest of guests.

ABOVE: The upstairs billiards room has elaborately carved Gothic-inspired panels and a custom carpet woven for the space.

FACING TOP: Custom walnut bookcases with special shelf lighting hold a collection of leather books in the library. The beautiful chandelier and wall sconces add a soft glow to the room.

FACING BOTTOM: An early French inlay desk is displayed in the center of the room on a custom carpet designed and created for the room.

ABOVE: A gorgeous carved mahogany mantelpiece was designed and created for the family living room, which is also paneled in mahogany. We recovered wing chairs from a previous residence and placed them on either side of the fireplace.

FACING: French doors lead to a covered terrace from the family living room. Door hardware is custom, by P.E. Guerin.

FACING: One of the first purchases, long before we broke ground for the house, was this glazed terra-cotta Italian fountain, which was outfitted as a vanity for one of the downstairs bathrooms. Walls were custom painted in a fantasy marble pattern.

ABOVE: A vestibule off the rotunda leads to an outdoor terrace. We used an unlined embroidered sheer to dress the top of the French doors. The console and mirror are antique.

IV
Major Home Additions Just for Collections

Many times a lovely home becomes overpowered by a collection. Suddenly the homeowners find they are not living with and enjoying the collection, but it has taken over the entire house and their lives. This can be a real problem with couples when only one of them is the collector. If the collector in the family collects something the other members don't care for—well, you probably know where I'm going with this. At this point, conversations start about housing the collection in an addition to the house—be it a room or an entire wing. Here is where the real work begins and hopefully an architect is hired. A seamless addition that enhances the original house is always preferable to an unattractive carbuncle of an add-on. This goes for not only the exterior, but the interior. A seamless flow from the old house to the new addition should be your goal. Always try and match the original building materials, both inside and out. The greatest compliment I get is when a visitor does not know, or cannot tell, what was original and what was added on.

"Replace two second-rate pieces
with one first-rate."

A Family Wing in the Georgian Style

When their original Georgian-style house got a little crowded, these clients decided to add on a wing for family living and entertaining and displaying collections. And add on we did—in a big way. The new large double-height rooms are spacious and can easily accommodate family activities and entertaining on a large scale. Two custom games tables can be put together quite easily to create a large banquet table. The vast family entertaining room is finished all in walnut; however, since the natural walnut was a little too dark, we bleached it all to create a mellow medium brown. Custom-designed bronze chandeliers light the room. The color choices came from the large area rug and the furniture plan is comfortable and inviting.

Upon arrival in the family wing entry, you are surrounded with multiple unique collections of artwork and decorative objects, and yet lots of family activity is always going on somewhere close by. It is a very livable house that is also filled with collection after collection—some light-hearted and fun and others quite serious.

FACING: A monumental, double-height family living room is paneled in walnut that has been lightened to a warm medium-brown. I designed the three bronze chandeliers, created by Lost Arts, for the room. They illuminate both the space below and the lovely plaster ceiling above.

ABOVE: The wing that houses the family living was seamlessly added onto the original Georgian-style residence. The architects were Richard Giegengack of Washington, D.C., and D. C. Broadstone of Dallas, Texas.

ABOVE LEFT: A view from the entry down a wide hallway leading into the family living room. Note the collection of vintage Steiff Bears on wheels.

ABOVE RIGHT: An antique octagonal table dominates the center of the family wing entry. A lovely old corner cabinet holds a collection of Chinese export porcelain and antique brass mortar and pestles.

FACING ABOVE: The other side of the room has two large, square games tables that can be combined to create a banquet-size dining table for entertaining in a big way. An antique snooker table with heavily carved legs is placed at one end of the room. A set of eight George III side chairs, upholstered in a whimsical cotton fabric, are scattered around the room.

FACING BELOW: A Regency rosewood and elm sofa table holds a collection of silver match cases. There is a similar table behind the other sofa and each has a good reading lamp. Comfort was a priority since it is the family living room.

FACING AND ABOVE LEFT: This 19th-century French oak cathedral is one of several of the owner's collections of antique models placed around the room. This handsome Gothic model needed a custom base, which we designed and had built with Gothic details to complement the model. I love the way the window treatments frame it!

ABOVE RIGHT: This charming French townhouse also has a custom base that complements the architecture of the house. These engaging models bring a lot of character to the room. Why do I always want to put a bird in one of them?

OVERLEAF: The dark-paneled sitting room (original to the house), or the "Churchill room," is a comfortable place to relax and enjoy the collection of Churchill memorabilia. The monumental bust of Churchill commands one end of the room while cozy wing chairs upholstered in F. Schumacher sit by the fireplace.

CHURCHILL

The "Churchill" room displays paintings by Winston Churchill as well as one of his artist palettes in a specially designed display pedestal. I must confess that Mr. Churchill with his cane has scared the life out of me on several occasions!

A Private Library and Art Gallery

A referral from a good friend of another client of mine landed me another dream job. It's funny how all these connections are made and you just never know who may like your work or your personality, or maybe it was just dumb luck!

I love clients who are really big thinkers and doers. They never cease to amaze me with their imagination and larger-than-life dreams, plus their ability to make it happen. One such client shared with me his dream of having a private library. Originally, it was going to be a separate building, but somehow it ended up as a large addition to the original house. Again, a wonderful team of very talented professionals including several architects and engineers, the contractor, and a huge team of specialists and consultants labored a very long time in planning and designing and constructing this new wing.

There was to be an art gallery on two levels, a large private office with adjoining rooms for assistants and a beautiful double-height private library. Did I say the client is a collector in every sense of the word? Well, it is true. Books, manuscripts, antiques, artwork, and significant historical documents began arriving every day and were stored for future installation. We actually created templates of much of the artwork, which we placed on the interior wall elevations, allowing us to come up with multiple options for the arrangements of the paintings. The art gallery rooms were done in a light painted finish. I decided to upholster the walls of the art gallery in a small, geometric-patterned fabric that would be forgiving of nail holes for future rehanging of the artwork, and the library was done entirely in rich, dark mahogany wood with ebony and gold accents. Special bookcases and cabinets were designed and built to house all of these wonderful treasures. The interior design involved selection and layout of the furniture, artwork, and all of the finishes, fabrics, lighting, and carpets throughout the wing. Truly, for me, it was the job of a lifetime.

When I visit now, I can hardly believe I got to work on such a fabulous project with such wonderful clients and so many, many talented craftspeople. It is always a joy to visit the library, and, yes, the treasures and new collections are still arriving.

ABOVE: The double-height library with its numerous bays for books is entered from the art gallery. An elaborate wood floor inlay is featured in the space between two oriental carpets.

FACING: A Regency portfolio stand is prominently displayed in one of the library bays. Everyone needs one of these to hold all of their artwork that hasn't been framed. I enjoyed designing the silk window treatments framing the view to the side terrace.

A specially built vitrine displays and protects historical letters and documents, which are changed out regularly. There is also a fabric cover that protects the contents from the light.

FACING: Abraham Lincoln's desk and chair from the U.S. House of Representatives are on display, along with books pertaining to the president's life.

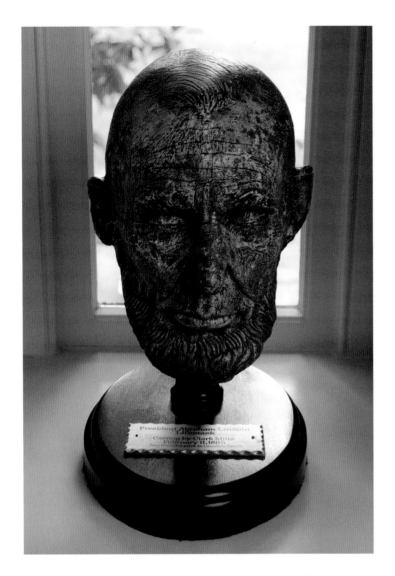 

ABOVE LEFT: A life mask of President Abraham Lincoln sits on a deep window ledge in a connecting hallway outside the private office.

ABOVE RIGHT: Framed miniature portraits are arranged between two windows in one corner of the octagonal private office. I had two of my favorite local artists, Brian Jones and Brian Scott, paint the trompe l'oeil ribbons on the wall.

FACING: The library has a raised stage for performances, complete with a Steinway concert grand, at the opposite end from the fireplace in the stately room.

OVERLEAF: This view reveals the enormous length of the main room of the library with its massive fluted mahogany columns and beautiful ornate plaster ceiling. The yellow damask parcel-gilt walnut armchair, in the foreground next to the sofa, is early 18th century.

The separate front entrance to the library wing has a very subtle, yet elegant, limestone floor and a sweeping limestone staircase. The new flooring of the addition is a perfect match to the limestone of the original (1917) house. The two hall chairs are English Regency period.

The art gallery, straight ahead from the entrance hall, holds a collection of 18th- and 19th-century paintings, furniture and sculptures. One of my personal favorites is the large painting on the right of three members of the Drummond family (1781) by Benjamin West. The antique center table is opposite the doorway into the library.

Sitting areas are plentiful throughout the art gallery, and guests are encouraged to sit and enjoy the collection, such as this painting by Charles Wilson Peale.

FACING: A portrait of George Washington by Rembrandt Peale is hung over an antique demilune cabinet.

ABOVE: Another important presidential portrait of Thomas Jefferson hangs over an Edwardian, ormolu-mounted, mahogany and oak vitrine table, an ideal display area for small precious objects.

The upper level of the art gallery displays more personal family paintings and unique collections of sculpture and decorative objects.

FACING: The enfilade is seen from the octagonal private office looking back through the art gallery to the entry door. The cords and tassels around the oval paintings are trompe l'oeil.

ABOVE: The octagonal private office has custom carpet and a magnificent crystal chandelier that I had great fun designing and having created for the handsome domed room. Collectibles come and go and are often placed on the deep window sills to enjoy. The elegant curtains soften the windows and frame the garden views.

"Collecting is preserving for the future."

ABOVE: A special wooden cabinet was designed to display the front and back of a very rare document relating to Mt. Vernon, the home of George Washington.

FACING: The enormous carved-mahogany fireplace, with its onyx-faced clock, dominates one end of the library's main room. A richly colored oriental carpet anchors a comfortable seating area. Multiple collections are displayed on antique tables and consoles.

An exquisite display cabinet is in the center of one of the smaller side rooms. The glass inset shows a collection of antique swords. Drawers lined with fabric can be opened to reveal other smaller collections.

A Southern Colonial for Art Collectors

Sometimes I get to live my dream through my clients. In this case I was lucky enough to get to renovate a wonderful old Southern colonial! Thank goodness for smart, brave clients who didn't want to tear this old beauty down, but sought to bring it back to life. I remember the day they called me and told me they had put a contract on the house and wanted me to see it and tell them if they were crazy. I couldn't wait to get there. The grounds were overgrown and we needed a machete to make our way through the dense vegetation, but through the moonlight I could get a faint glimpse of the white columns of the magnificent antebellum porch. Actually, it was daytime and I think I am confusing what really happened with a scene from *Gone with the Wind* or maybe *Hush . . . Hush, Sweet Charlotte*. Anyway, we made our way up the porch and through the wonderful old front doors into a fabulous entry with a lovely curving staircase. A spacious dining room was on the right and an exquisite living room with a perfect original fireplace mantel was to our left. Straight ahead was the most awful old family room from the '50s you have ever seen. We shouldn't have gone that far, I guess. (Eventually, we just tore it off and replaced it with a seamless addition.) It didn't matter, because I was so excited and I think I got them excited and off we went—with the help of a talented architect and a great contractor—on a big redo and a huge adventure.

I had visions of Greek revival even though the house was not old enough to be technically Greek revival. However, it had several touches of it, with the pediments over the interior doorways and those lovely columns outside, which we could play up. We could always—and we did—add a few more touches with moldings and stenciled anthemions and Greek keys on the wood floors here and there and everywhere. Oh, was it ever fun!

The clients had toured a lot of old plantation houses in the South and had become fascinated with the idea of a *garçonnière*, or outbuilding close to the main house, which in its original intent was used to house unruly teenage boys and keep them away from any unmarried women who might be staying in the big house. (Disclaimer: the clients do have a son, but he certainly wasn't unruly and didn't have any bearing on the building of the *garçonnière*!) These small structures were usually architecturally interesting and often octagonal in shape. We decided it might be fun to build one in the front of the house facing the garden for a guest-house. Another version would be in the back as a summerhouse. When it was almost complete the husband thought he had gone too far and was ready to tear it down, but he came around and it was completed. I found a lovely bedroom set of old painted cottage furniture, and we dolled it up with linen fabrics and hooked rugs and now they can hardly get rid of the guests.

I almost forgot that the clients had quite the collection of contemporary artwork; however, the clients were young and cute and I was determined to make this house fresh and not a museum. I asked for only one or two antique pieces per room with lots of comfortable upholstery and then we topped it off with their wonderful collection of contemporary art. We housed collections of lovely Bristol glass in an antique secretary, and we displayed the client's extensive collection of majolica and Palissy ware on the walls of the breakfast room. I used the softest, lightest shades of pale blue and pale green and yellow for wall colors and kept the polished wood floors mostly bare. Elegant silk curtains could float in the breeze from any open window. Oops, I forgot this is Texas; our only breeze is from the air-conditioning.

The original mantel was saved and restored and two gilt bronze sconces were added, leaving room for artwork in the center. I designed the elegant lounge chairs to be pretty from the front, back or side, as comfortable seating next to the fireplace. A few antique pieces, such as the painted stool, were added for character.

The living room's original plaster walls were restored and painted the softest pastel shade of green. Custom upholstery is comfortable with the occasional antique chair thrown in, as well as a modern silver leaf tea table. The large painting over the sofa is by John Alexander.

The family room, with its upholstery fabrics in yellows and greens, is grounded by a large antique Oushak rug. The wall behind the sofa holds a David Bates painting. Tables scattered around the room were chosen for their unique styles.

ABOVE: I asked the clients for one antique piece in each room. We found an elegant secretary for the living room and filled it with a few special collections like Bristol glass and Parian vases. The floors were left bare to show off the lovely stenciled border.

FACING: We found this charming and useful antique buffet for the breakfast room. The shelves hold many of the wife's collection of cookbooks, and we topped it off with an arrangement of majolica. New crisp linen slipcovers were recently added to the antique breakfast room chairs.

FACING: A solid block of marble was carved to create this special soaking tub in the master bath. Getting it installed was certainly another story! A pair of antique bronze wall sconces accent the side walls of the tub alcove.

ABOVE: A magnificent Jim Dine *Venus de Milo* sculpture is framed by a pair of pilasters at the end of the gallery leading to the library and the master suite. Wonderful artwork makes all the difference and is such a joy to display and arrange. French doors open to the garden.

A Residence for Entertaining
with a Collections Wing

I received a call to visit a potential client in a lovely home that was overflowing with art and collections. (She had seen another of my projects for a major collector—referrals are always best!) She and her husband had decided to remodel the house and add a huge addition for entertaining and for the display of even more collections. Both being avid collectors, as well as passionate entertainers, they needed additional space for events hosted in their home. The house was traditional in design, as would be the addition, and the goal was an elegant, livable home, in which it would be easy to entertain large groups for dinners or concerts. Pulling off a dinner for one hundred people should be easy and one shouldn't have to move out all the existing furniture. Right? So that was our goal.

Working with the architect, we enlarged the original living and dining rooms and added a large room for concerts or dinner parties. Lots of attention was given to the size of the rooms and the number of people who could be accommodated for parties or for seated dinners. A new staircase was added along with wonderfully wide hallways for display of artwork. Storage for tables and chairs and all things needed for hosting a large event was also given top priority. Many new built-ins for collections and custom display cabinets were added in the collections wing as well as a pair of lovely corner cabinets in the dining room for antique silver.

One of my proudest contributions was the color scheme. A perfect shade of yellow warmed up the entry and was carried down the major hallways leading first-time guests to the music room and also creating an attractive background along the way for the paintings and antique furniture pieces.

Again, this project wasn't completed in six weeks—more like several years! There were hundreds of meetings and lots and lots of details. We worked with an excellent architect, lighting designer, builder, and many talented artists and craftsmen.

The soft yellow walls of the massive entrance hall are a warm backdrop to the collection of Dutch artwork and 18th-century French walnut commodes. The entrance has beautiful openings leading to the sitting room and dining room or straight ahead to a central hallway.

The dining room, with a large Edwardian dining table and a Sheraton sideboard (ca. 1760) has walls upholstered in an elegant damask by Jasper Fabrics. Antique paintings and silver are displayed throughout the spacious room. A magnificent bronze and crystal chandelier hangs over the table and is reflected in the large, oval French mirror.

An overview of the sitting room, with blue silk walls by Stark as a soft background for a pair of lovely antique French mirrors and a pair of 7th-century Chinese terra-cotta figures. The stunning coromandel screen (with five panels here and five more on the other side of the room) is late 17th century.

The floating staircase was created as part of the renovation and addition. Holly Hall was the architect. All the additional floor space gave us a new opportunity for display of artwork and sculpture. The stair runner is from Stark Carpets.

FACING: A view from the upstairs landing looking down onto the round center table holding an early Chinese earthenware camel (618-907 AD). A wonderful chance to view the sculpture from all angles presents itself as one ascends the stairs.

FACING: A partial view of the dining room shows one of the custom corner cabinets designed to display a portion of the owner's extensive collection of antique silver from the 1800s. The sixteen walnut dining chairs are George III.

ABOVE: A silver tea service sits underneath an early 17th-century Dutch portrait.

OVERLEAF: The living room is impressive with a 17th-century Dutch still life and a collection of Chinese terra-cotta infantry soldiers (circa 220 B.C.) on the mantel. The antique carpet is from Abrash Antique Rugs.

FACING: A western room, with walls of antique firearms and an important collection of items belonging to General Custer, including his saddle and rifle. The painting is a famous battle scene.

ABOVE: A section of one of several walls of custom built-ins for display of antique rifles and pistols. The cabinetry was faux grained to resemble mahogany and the backs were upholstered in green wool. Special iron hooks were fabricated to hold the firearms in place. Note the enormous and very heavy slab of petrified wood in the center. That was no easy installation!

The Art and How-To
of Displaying a Collection

I started collecting for myself in my late twenties and over the intervening years have helped other people make space for, design, and arrange their own collections. So, I feel like I have some expert insights to share.

I have never had to sit and think about what I wanted to collect. I was just naturally interested in a particular this or that and starting buying them, sometimes not even realizing that I had started another collection. If I had to make a conscious effort to start a collection now, I would probably tie it into something for the home that I would enjoy looking at and that would be fun to decorate with.

As with most people, the shape, color, and material always catch my attention first and probably has a lot to do with whether I start collecting it or not. Art is a great example of something that is easily collected and doesn't always have to be expensive, but it certainly can enhance your home and your life. Wonderful original watercolors are available at consignment stores, flea markets and estate sales and are usually very good deals. Photographs or maps or engravings are also easy to find and can be the beginning of a great collection. The collection will be easier to display and will look better if you stick with one medium. (Just imagine a wall in your living room covered with black-and-white engravings in gold frames, or black-and-white photographs in simple white frames.) What about a wall of silhouettes? I started with my own that was done when I was a little boy and then started collecting cutouts of other people.

I like to collect things I can use—like dishes and tabletop pieces. Find a pattern you love or a type of porcelain, like Imari or Chinese export or even Melmac. Silver flatware is a great collectible—beautiful, usable and a good investment. If Grandmother didn't leave you any silver, just start your own pattern. (And don't tell me you don't want anything you'd have to polish. If you take care of it correctly, you rarely have to polish it.) What about stemware? Find a pattern you love to look at and enjoy drinking your cocktail or your ice tea from. America has had great glass factories that have produced beautiful glassware. I love Heisey, especially their Greek Key pattern. You can find glasses, ice buckets, serving dishes, small plates and almost anything else you can imagine. (I love using my Greek Key pattern for cocktail parties.) Use it and mix it up with your other things!

Always buy the best you can afford. We all love a "find," but sometimes you have to really pay for that special piece. I think it all averages out in the end. Don't let your collection get away from you. Sometimes it's not about quantity—although, at the beginning I suffer from that. More is more and when does enough become too much? (Collecting is one thing and hoarding is another.) It's good to evaluate what you have and then edit and upgrade. Sell a few of your pieces and invest in better examples.

One of the best things about collecting is learning something new about something you maybe didn't know much about. Most collectors love to talk and share their knowledge. The internet makes it easy to research and see examples. Museums often have the best examples and visits can help to sharpen your eye and increase your knowledge.

Putting thought into how you display your collection is also very important. Many collectors have fabulous things, but they are so unorganized and poorly displayed or lighted that I don't know how their owners can enjoy them or appreciate them. Buy a display cabinet for your collection, or build some shelving, or add some good lighting for your wall of artwork. At the very least, take it out of the boxes if you have it stored away and put it out to enjoy! If you are tired of it, get rid of it and start a new collection!

Displaying a Collection

I consider the display of a collection to be a large part of my job as the interior designer. Hopefully, in planning the new house or the addition, the owners and their design team have adequately addressed the space needed for the collection. (As with most collectors, there is never enough space.) Long before construction is started, the amount of wall space and floor space for display cabinets and shelving should be decided. There are always changes along the way and hopefully improvements to the original design. Walls where unusually heavy items are to be hung should be blocked for the additional weight. Upholstering of walls or the backs of cases should also have been done. The lighting should be in place. When the dust settles, hopefully, the move-in starts and the magic begins.

Over the years I have picked up several ideas on how to make a collection look its best and the most important items to think about when displaying a collection.

Installing the Collection

Many collectibles need special hangers or mounts to be able to be displayed properly. Often these have to be custom-made to the size or shape of the object. The finish of these hangers or mounts should not detract from the object itself.

Everything looks more important on a special base or pedestal. These can be made of many different materials including wood, metal, or acrylic, to name a few. It is important that the size be appropriate for the item being displayed as well as placed at the best height for viewing.

Custom display cases can be created to display and protect a collection. They can be lined in fabric, have adjustable shelves, have glass or acrylic tops that open, and, of course, be lit to enhance the collection.

ABOVE: This amazing display cabinet was custom built for *Noah's Ark* and all the animals created out of semiprecious stones. I worked directly with the artist on the design and lighting requirements.

FACING: Acrylic is wonderful for creating pedestals with protective covers that allow full view of the objects being displayed. These kraters (circa 380 B.C.) almost appear to be floating above the stairs.

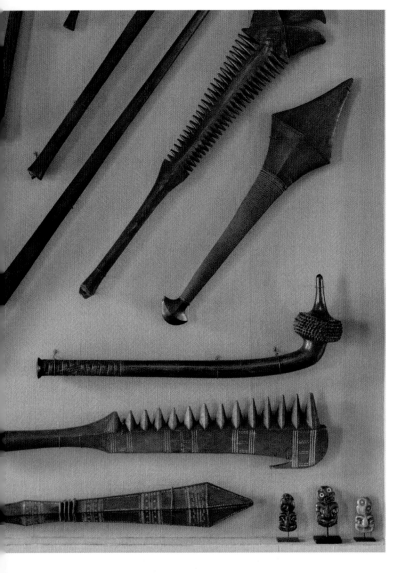

To arrange this collection of African clubs, I made a template the size of the display wall and laid out all of the clubs on the floor to determine the most pleasing arrangement. It was photographed and then used as a guide for the actual installation. Special holders were fabricated for each object. The room and most of the clubs are made of wood, so the blue fabric was selected to contrast with all of the brown.

FACING: Custom mahogany bases were designed and built for each of the bronzes on display in the client's home office. They fit perfectly in the spaces between the windows.

Arranging by Shape and Size

Before actually hanging the pieces on the wall or inside of a cabinet I will often lay them out on a large piece of paper cut to the size of the display area. There it becomes much easier to move the items around into the most aesthetically pleasing arrangement. Here is the tricky part—I guess there is no rule—I trust my eye for the most attractive combination of shapes and sizes.

ABOVE: A set of white marble relief panels of Roman emperors is stacked and hung three-over-three in a stair landing. They are hung slightly higher than standing eye level.

FACING: Hanging art around one central object—here, an open-back wall shelf—can be very interesting to the eye. This arrangement shows off two different collections.

ABOVE LEFT: Marble Roman fragments (first-to-second-century B.C.) are placed on brackets and arranged in an asymmetrical composition on a wall of coral-colored Venetian plaster. This complicated layout and install owes a large debt to the design eye of Jordan McAdams and her fabulous team.

ABOVE RIGHT: A set of Hogarth prints artfully arranged over a small demilune console makes this hallway a lot more fun to walk through.

FACING: An intriguing arrangement of "pairs" of unrelated objects makes for a charming composition above this bed. The ribbons with bows unify and add a decorative touch. Most of these items were inherited, and the client had a sentimental attachment to each one.

Background Colors, Fabrics, and Textures

The softness, texture, sheen, and certainly the color of a fabric placed behind or in back of a collection can make all the difference in terms of an attractive display. The color of the fabric is probably the most important decision and should definitely enhance the collection in the best way possible. It has to be just right: not too strong as to overpower, but not too weak that it is a waste of time to even install.

A client who collects vintage Waterford stemware needed storage and display in their new wine-tasting room. A colorful stipple-pattern wallpaper was chosen to line the backs of the cabinets, and glass shelves with interior lighting were added.

FACING: A collection of Staffordshire dogs and lions is displayed in what had been a bookcase. Glass shelves and an accent color painted on the back were added to highlight the porcelains. It was an easy fix for a client who needed display and not bookcases.

ABOVE: The built-in cabinet (one of two in the room) was lined in a blue linen fabric to create a backdrop for both books and art objects. The blue is a nice contrast with the books and the bronzes. The right color can make all the difference.

ABOVE: Formerly white bookcases were faux grained to resemble walnut and accented with a rich blue paint to highlight a beautiful collection of majolica and English brass-bound lap desks that the clients have assembled over forty years of travel and collecting.

FACING: A collection of English porcelain becomes a focal point in this sitting room. A special strié paint with glaze finish on the back and sides of the arched cabinet accents the dinner set.

Acquired Furniture Pieces or Cabinets for Collections

This is one of the easiest ways to show off a collection. Finding a wonderful old cupboard or armoire or breakfront and turning it into a home for a collection can solve many challenges. It certainly saves the time and money to design and build custom display pieces. Upholster the back of the piece in fabric, paint it, or even wallpaper the back. Add lighting and you are all set up.

FACING: An unusual and important Art Nouveau display cabinet holds a collection of porcelains from the same time period. It was decided early on that the guest suite would have an Art Nouveau theme. The objects and designs are fascinating.

ABOVE: A late 18th-century oak dresser holds a collection of horn and bone objects plus two large ironstone pieces on the bottom shelf. It adds so much character to a hallway leading outdoors. Why not enjoy your collections each time you pass by?

ABOVE: My grandmother's old brown wood secretary, in all its faux-grained glory, holds my collection of Chinese export porcelain and mudmen. I love the glass upper section and all the cubby-holes for display and, of course, the "secret" door that everyone knows about!

FACING: One of a pair of Edwardian mahogany and ormolu-mounted vitrines holding a collection of small enamel treasures. These unique pieces can be found at auctions and estate sales and can be a collector's best friend!

ABOVE: An unusual mahogany and satinwood English cabinet placed at the end of a long hallway entices visitors with its collection of antique silver hollowware for hot beverages. The vase pattern on the glass doors is quite charming.

FACING: A delightful four-tier revolving book table is perfect for floating in the center of a room and displaying collections of "smalls." Weren't cabinetmakers clever?

Custom Lighting for the Collection

One of the most important parts of displaying a great collection to its best advantage, and not one of the easiest, is lighting. It usually requires a professional who can determine the best type of lighting. I would recommend talking with a lighting consultant. Recessed lighting or surface-mounted ceiling lights (such as track lighting) can do the job and give you more flexibility. Shelf lighting or strip lighting inside the cabinets or shelving requires a lot of planning and proper installation. New advancements in lighting with less heat output and energy waste have given us so many more options. It is important not to over-light or damage the collection with too much lighting. Natural light from windows and openings can also be very damaging and requires appropriate window treatments or filming of the glass to protect against harmful UV rays. As much as we all love the sun, it isn't always a friend to your collection.

FACING: Custom strip lighting was installed inside this elaborate dining room corner cabinet to highlight the owner's impressive collection of colorful and very ornate porcelains.

ABOVE: Brass picture lights installed above the bookcases softly wash the books with light.

Special lighting for the bookshelves and display cabinets is not only aesthetically pleasing but helps when searching for a specific book or reading a plaque relating to an item's description. Note the special lighting under each shelf in the medal cabinet.

LEFT: A whimsical Clementine Hunter painting is illuminated with a dedicated recessed art light installed in the ceiling. A collection of American cut glass is displayed below.

RIGHT: Sometimes natural light is the best, as with this collection of porcelain glove molds sitting in a deep windowsill. I have collected these for years and they always make me laugh. Probably says more about me than the molds!

"Love it and light it or lose it"

LEFT: An example of successful lighting is seen in this display of Staffordshire and Imari. The soft coral linen fabric complements the porcelains and contrasts with the charcoal color paint of the cabinet.

RIGHT: Display cabinets lining the walls of this collector's room are filled with some of nature's most unusual and beautiful creations. Glass shelves, shown in this section, allow the light to bathe each geode perfectly.

OVERLEAF: The boat room is a special space designed to accommodate a collection of memorabilia from the *Titanic* as well as a number of antique maps. I proposed the unique barrel-vault ceiling and molding details to suggest the interior of a boat. Recessed ceiling lighting highlights each wall grouping. The clients often use the room to plan their trips or enjoy photo albums of past sea adventures.

Epilogue

I think everyone should collect something. I usually tell clients that; sometimes they do and sometimes they don't. However, the ones that do seem to catch on quite quickly and off we go! I have been so lucky to help in the acquisition of collections, deciding how to edit and organize, and, finally, to decorate rooms, wings, or whole houses with magnificent collections of just about anything and everything you can imagine. Even once, a twelve-hundred-pound Arctic muskox, alas, never photographed. But that's a story for another time.

Acknowledgments

I have enjoyed writing this book, but I certainly could not have accomplished it by myself. There were so many people who helped me along the way.

First, I needed something that inspired me to write about and photograph. And for that I am thankful for the many, many wonderful clients over the years who have allowed me to help them with their homes and collections and have also given me permission to photograph their residences. Without that, we certainly wouldn't have a book. I am so grateful for the friendships that have developed and the fun projects that I was lucky enough to be a part of. Each and every one of you have my sincere thanks for trusting in me and allowing me to be a part of the design of your most special place—your home.

When I came up with the concept of the book, I shared it first with James Campbell, my biggest fan and promoter and the person I share so much with. He was, and has always been, enthusiastic about everything I do and loves design and collecting as much, or more than, I do.

Once I started to gather my ideas about a book on collecting and to organize photos of my projects, I turned to Valerie Cain, my longtime project manager, whose taste and organizational skills I have long admired in my office. She helped me to put my first thoughts and photos into a format that were the beginnings of a possible book. I could not have done it without her valuable help and input.

I thank my editor, Madge Baird, whose gentle guidance and encouragement kept me going and on the right track in making the book a reality.

None of my projects could have ever been accomplished without the talented help of so many wonderful artists, drapery workrooms, upholsterers, painters, installers and craftsmen. They have always been a valuable part of my work family and I am so grateful for their help and loyalty.

I thank the many talented architects, builders and consultants who have been a part of the team on these many projects. You have my respect and admiration.

Finally, I thank the photographers who captured the essence of my projects and preserved them with these beautiful images. I enjoyed all the photo shoots and am grateful for your talent and patience—especially that time when the dog bit us!

A collection of cut glass decanters is displayed and used in this colorful living room filled with beautifully upholstered seating.

Project Credits

Architects

Larry E. Boerder
Larry E. Boerder Architects
www.larryboerder.com

D.C. Broadstone II
www.dcbarchitect.com

Richard Drummond Davis
www.rddavisarchitect.com

Richard Giegengack

Holly Hall, architect
HPD Architecture
www.hpdarch.com

George Hopkins
The Hopkins Co.
www.hopkinsco.com

Clay Nelson
C.A. Nelson, Architects
www.canelsonarchitects.com

Deric Salser

Debra Settle
D. Settle, Architect
www.dsettlearchitect.com

Builders

Ed Jarrett & Son LLC
www.theedjarrettcompany.com

Steven Hild Custom Builder
www.hildcustombuilder.net

Lloyd Construction Consultants

Sebastian Construction Group
www.sebastiancg.com

Lighting Consultants

Steven Byrdwaters, Byrdwaters Design
www.byrdwaters.com

Kevin Fitzgerald, Fox Electric
www. foxelectric.com

Curtis Liberda, 2CLighting
www.2clighting.net

Scott Oldner, Oldner Lighting
www.oldnerlighting.com

Photographers

Dallas Visual Design
pages 136, 137, 146–49, 153, 156–59, 165, 198

Steve Foxal
www.stevefoxallphotography.com
pages 202, 204 left, 217

Michael Hunter
www.michaelhunterphotography.com
pages 2-15, 26–47, 49, 51–53, 60–95, 177, 180–196, 199–201, 203, 204 right–211, 213–214, 216, 222 left, 223, 226

Stephen Karlisch, Karlisch Photography
www.karlischstudio.com
pages 48, 50, 170–76, 178–79, 222 right

Geno Loro
www.genoloro.com
pages 116–33, 212, 218

Nancy Nolan Photography
www.nancynolanphotography.com
pages 16–23

Dan Piassick
www.piassick.com
pages 96–115, 138–45, 150–152, 154-55, 160-64, 166–69, 215, 220–21, 224–25